ANTON RUBINSTEIN
Piano Music

Selected and with an Introduction by
Joseph Banowetz

DOVER PUBLICATIONS, INC.
Mineola, New York

To my good friend David Dubal,
extraordinary pianist, author,
and fellow lover of pianism
in the Romantic tradition.

Bibliographical Note

This Dover edition, first published in 2001, is a new compilation of works originally published separately in early authoritative editions. Joseph Banowetz's introduction was prepared specially for this collection.

International Standard Book Number: 0-486-41380-2

Manufactured in the United States of America
Dover Publications, Inc., 31 East 2nd Street, Mineola, N.Y. 11501

CONTENTS

Ondine 1
Étude, Op. 1 (1842)

Melody in F. 5
No. 1 of *Deux Mélodies,* Op. 3 (1852)

Kamennïy-ostrov 9
No. 22 from *Kamennïy-ostrov* [Rocky Island]: *Album de* [24] *Portraits,*
Op. 10 (1853–4)

Barcarolle in G minor 16
No. 3 of *Six Pièces caractéristiques,* Op. 50 (1854–8)

Romance in E-flat. 20
No. 1 of six *Soirées á Saint-Petersbourg,* Op. 44 (1860)

Impromptu in E-flat 23
No. 4 from *Album de Peterhof:* * *Douze Morceaux,* Op. 75 (1866)

Mazurka *(Pologne)* 27
No. 4 of eight pieces in *Album de Danses populaires*
des différentes Nations, Op. 82 (1868)

Lezghinka *(Caucase)* 34
No. 1 from *Album de Danses populaires des différentes Nations*

"El Dachtarawan": Marche orientale 43
No. 7 from *Miniatures: 12 Morceaux,* Op. 93, Book 9 (1872–3)

Akrostichon II. 46
No. 2 of five pieces in *Deuxième Akrostichon,* Op. 114 (1890)

Polonaise in E-flat minor 51
The last of *Souvenir de Dresde: Six Morceaux,* Op. 118 (1894)

*Peterhof, Rubinstein's summer retreat, lay outside St. Petersburg, on the Gulf of Finland. His *Album de Peterhof* is a musical picture album of family memories and impressions of this favorite place.

INTRODUCTION

Anton Rubinstein (1829–1894), whose playing helped shape an entire generation of pianists, was a titanic force of pianism throughout 19th-century Russia and Europe. As an educator alone, he spearheaded the entire conservatory system in Russia with his founding of St. Petersburg Conservatory in 1862. His most famous student, the legendary Josef Hofmann, would carry Rubinstein's pianistic tradition to the concert halls of the world for a half century after the master's death.

Although Rubinstein's seminal role as performer and educator is uncontested, his standing as a composer remains controversial to this day. The quality of his works is uneven, often stemming from an uncritical pen hastening to complete a piece in the heat of a momentary (or monetary!) inspiration. But to speak of his shortcomings is to ignore many works that reveal Rubinstein's extraordinary sensitivity to color, texture, and melodic shape. Astonishingly prolific, he produced 119 works with opus numbers and 70 without, including huge operas, oratorios, six symphonies, a violin concerto, and eight works for piano and orchestra.

One important caveat should be given to anyone playing Rubinstein. Like some of the works of Franz Liszt, Rubinstein's piano music can be easily spoiled by a mediocre, superficial performance that fails to seek beyond the surface of the score. In both composers, what may be branded as "empty" or "bombastic" is too often the victim of a reading that amounts to little more than showy glitter. Certain composers need special protection from such artistic maiming—and Rubinstein is clearly one of them. Under the right hands, his music has a charm and vitality that rewards the sensitive player.

PERFORMANCE SUGGESTIONS

Phrasing:

Long phrases are extremely important in this music; indeed, most great interpreters of the Romantic repertory tend to think in long melodic lines, much like a singer who does not have to breathe in short gasps.

For instance—in the *Impromptu,* Op. 75, No. 4 (p. 23)—keep the first eight measures as one phrase instead of "breathing" at the middle of the fourth measure. Rubinstein's dynamics perfectly reflect what must be done at the keyboard to maintain this long line.

The same long-line phrasing shapes the first twelve measures of the *Romance,* Op. 44, No. 1 (p. 20). Again, the composer's dynamics help the performer to project this to the audience.

A special instance of extended phrasing occurs in *El Dachtarawan* (p. 43), where longer groupings are formed by consecutive three-measure units with identical rhythms. Here, the first six measures should be held together, then linked to the next six, creating a long twelve-measure phrase. Those who heard Josef Hofmann play remarked that he, like Rubinstein himself, never repeated the same material in the same way, giving his interpretations a marvelous interest and aliveness. We can use this approach to hold together smaller units of phrasing.

Melodic projection:

From all accounts of Rubinstein's playing, a marvelous singing tone was one of his most notable features. Keep this in mind as you clearly project a melody over its accompanimental texture—especially if the melody is placed in the middle of surrounding figurations. Linked with a sense of long line, this sort of projection is one of the greatest aids in the best performances of Rubinstein's music.

Pedaling:

According to contemporary descriptions of his playing, Rubinstein must have been one the most imaginative masters of modern pedaling technique—indeed, he himself called the pedal no less than "the soul of the piano."

In Rubinstein's music, some players tend to think in smaller "bites" and "pockets" of pedal, not realizing that longer pedaling often gives more atmosphere and color to one's playing, especially on larger instruments and in a larger performance space. The famous *Kamennïy-ostrov,* Op. 10, No. 22 (p. 9), has possibilities for this pedaling approach. For instance, on p. 13, beginning at Tempo I, hold the pedal without interruption for seven measures, then change it only on the whole-note G-sharp. This kind of extended holding of the pedal for atmosphere can even be used through the very opening nine measures of the music. If you feel the onset of too much blurring, then make a half- or quarter-pedal change rather than an antiseptic full chop of the pedal.

One of the "secrets" of a convincing performance of these piano works is to maintain a richness of color and tone. A carefully chosen, often plentiful, use of pedal helps to achieve this.

Conquering large hand stretches:

Like most composer-pianists, Rubinstein wrote for his own hand—which, by all accounts, was gigantic. When you encounter a large reach, simply ask yourself if part of that chord or passage can be played with the other hand. This is not "cheating," especially when you realize that the composer himself could easily take these spans, and certainly would not have rolled them. If you *do* have to roll a chord, make the speed of the roll match the character and mood of the passage. (In a slow passage, for instance, avoid a jerky, rapid roll.) Try to "catch" all notes of a broken chord in the pedal and, to insure this, leave open the possibility of rolling a chord *on* the beat, not before it. Depending on context, a large chord can also be broken at some point rather than rolled from top to bottom. Experiment as the need arises. Go by what sounds good!

These few suggestions for learning and performing Rubinstein's piano music are by no means exhaustive. If applied wisely, however, they can make all the difference between a mediocre or flawed experience and a wonderful, musically satisfying performance. There are little gems to be found here for all who would seek them out among works that span the composer's creative life, from *Ondine* of 1842, his first published composition, to the *Polonaise,* Op. 118, No. 6, written the year of his death in 1894, and dedicated to his pupil Josef Hofmann. Of special interest is the inclusion of *El Dachtarawan* in an edition by Hofmann. Most of the music in this collection avoids advanced technical demands.

Joseph Banowetz
Dallas, Texas
June, 2000

ABOUT THE EDITOR

Joseph Banowetz has been described by Fanfare Record Review (U.S.) as "a giant among keyboard artists of our time," and by Russia's News (Moscow) as "a magnificent virtuoso." As recitalist, orchestral soloist, and recording artist of international critical acclaim, he has appeared on five continents. In addition to his recordings of concertos of Tchaikovsky, Liszt, and d'Albert, Mr. Banowetz has had released eight CDs of the music of Anton Rubinstein, including all eight works for piano and orchestra, as well as solo works. His world-premiere recording of Balakirev works received a German Music Critics' award as an Outstanding Record of the Year, and his recording of Rubinstein's Concertos Nos. 1 and 2 was given a similar citation in the United States by Fanfare. A graduate with a First Prize from the Vienna Academy for Music and Dramatic Arts, and a recipient of the Liszt Medal by the Hungarian Liszt Society, Mr. Banowetz has given lectures and masterclasses at The Juilliard School, St. Petersburg Conservatory, Royal College of Music, Beijing Central Conservatory, Shanghai Conservatory, and the Hong Kong Academy for the Performing Arts. Mr. Banowetz is a frequent guest on international piano juries, and his book *The Pianist's Guide to Pedaling* has been published in five languages. He is presently on the Artist-Faculty of the University of North Texas.

Ondine

Étude, Op. 1 (1842)

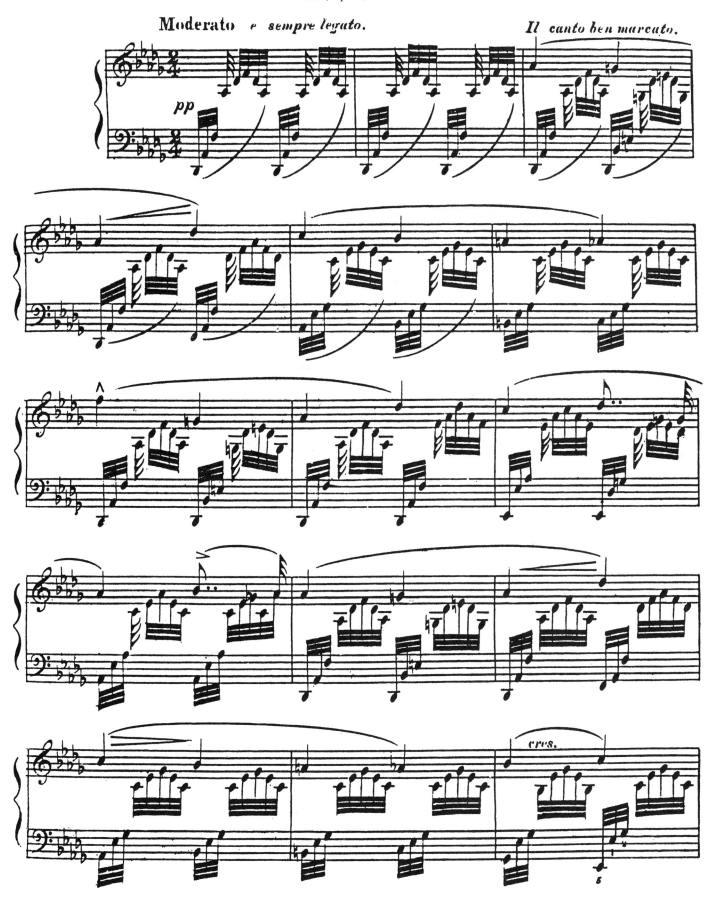

1

Melody in F

No. 1 of *Deux Mélodies* [Two Melodies], Op. 3 (1852)

Kamennïy-ostrov

No. 22 from *Kamennïy-ostrov*: *Album de* [24] *Portraits*

[Rocky Island: Portrait Album], Op. 10 (1853–4)

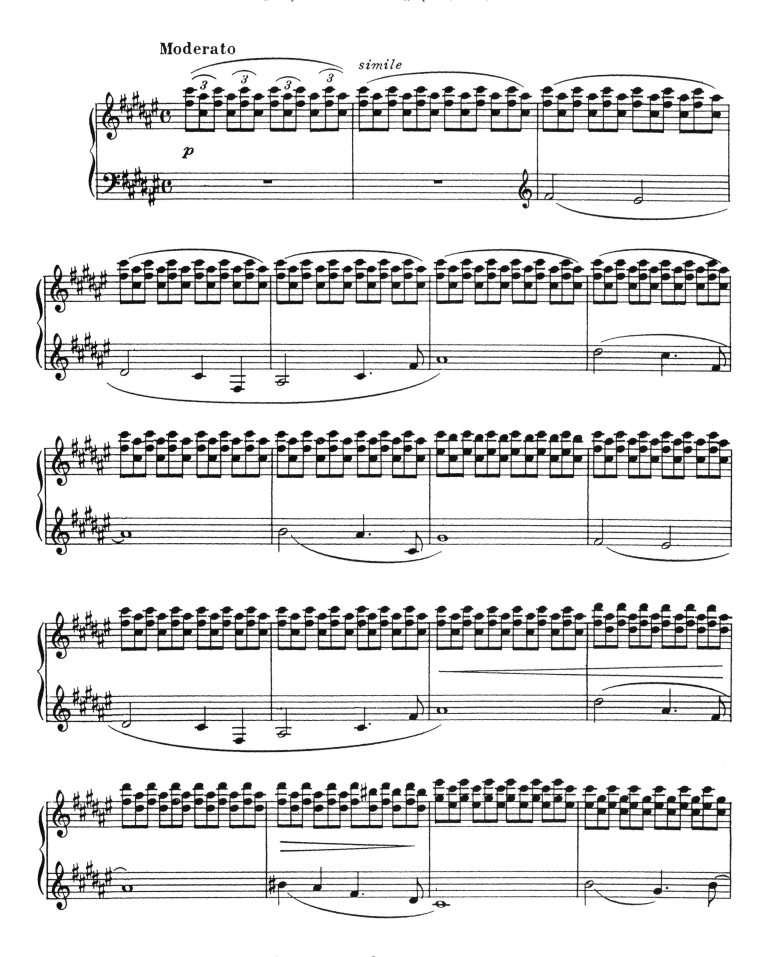

Tempo I

stringendo

Barcarolle in G minor

No. 3 of *Six Pièces caractéristiques* [Six Character Pieces]

Op. 50 (1854–8)

Andantino con moto.

Poco animato.

Romance in E-flat

No. 1 of six *Soirées á Saint-Petersbourg* [Evenings in St. Petersburg]

Op. 44 (1860)

Andante con moto

Impromptu in E-flat

No. 4 from *Album de Peterhof: Douze Morceaux*

[Peterhof Album: Twelve Pieces], Op. 75 (1866)

Mazurka
(Pologne / Poland)

No. 4 of eight pieces in *Album de Danses populaires des différentes Nations*

[Album of Popular Dances of Different Nations], Op. 82 (1868)

Lezghinka
(Caucase / Caucases)

No. 1 of eight pieces in *Album de Danses populaires des différentes Nations*
[Album of Popular Dances of Different Nations], Op. 82 (1868)

Allegro assal.

"El Dachtarawan"

Marche orientale

No. 7 from *Miniatures: 12 Morceaux* [12 Pieces], Op. 93, Book 9 (1872–3)

Revised and edited by Josef Hofmann

[The title is thought to be in Farsi, the language of Persia. Unfortunately,
it has eluded the editor's best efforts to discover its meaning.]

Akrostichon II

No. 2 of five pieces in *Deuxième Akrostichon* [Second Acrostic]

Op. 114 (1890)

Note: With the letter O prefacing this second piece of a set of five,
Rubinstein's "Acrostic" spells out the name of an unidentified SOFIA.

Polonaise in E-flat minor

The last of of *Souvenir de Dresde: Six Morceaux*

[Remembrance of Dresden: Six Pieces], Op. 118 (1894)

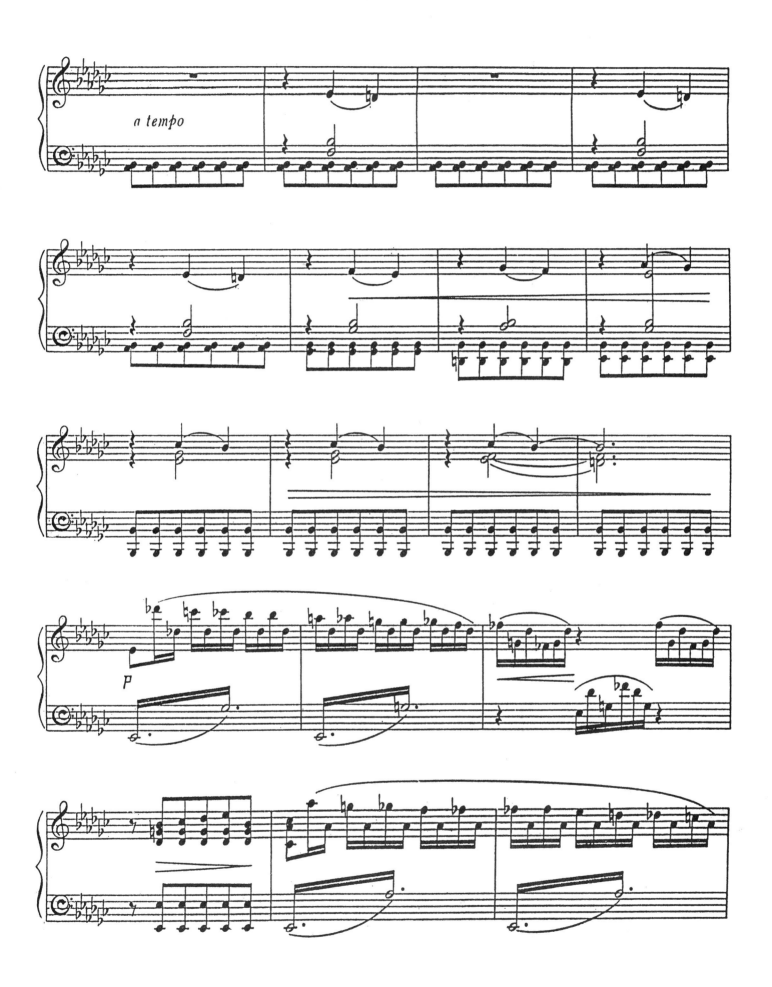